When You Listen For GOD'S Voice . . .

Life is Chile

Mateo WarSteiner

When You Listen for GOD's Voice . . . Life is Chile by Mateo WarSteiner

Self-Published by: Mateo WarSteiner
Cover Design by: Mateo WarSteiner
Editing by: Mateo WarSteiner

ISBN-13: 978-0-692233-73-3
ISBN-10: 0692233733
BISAC: Religion / Christian Life / Inspirational

10 9 8 7 6 5 4 3 2 1
First Edition
Printed in the United States of America

Dedicated to anyone searching for
the ever-present VOICE of the one true

God

"But from there you will seek the LORD your God and you will find Him, if you search after Him with all your heart and with all your soul. When you are in tribulation, and all these things come upon you in the latter days, you will return to the LORD your God and obey His VOICE."

Deuteronomy 4:29-30 (ESV)

Life is Chile

Peace to you, brothers and sisters in our redeemer Christ Jesus! Compelled by the Spirit, I have recorded my testimony to encourage your faith and share with you how God radically flipped my life upside down for the better. I know with all my heart, soul and mind, that He can change your life as well. The question is, are you willing to listen? Let me explain.

I've never heard a booming voice from the heavens. Most would assume that this would be the way the God of the universe would choose to address us, if He ever did so out loud. Yet He talks to us directly all the same. The problem is, *we're not listening!* It wasn't until my 25th lap around the sun that I finally even thought about listening.

The Bible teaches us that normal humans such as Adam and Moses actually had physical conversations with God. People tend to think that

1

since modern times, He has somehow distanced Himself from us because we aren't approached in the same manner. I'm here to tell you that He never left. In fact, God is just as close as He ever was before!

I want to be very honest with you. For starters, I'm not perfect, not even close. I'm not a preacher or a biblical scholar. Nor would anyone that knows me ever label me a saint. Haha! Had to laugh for a second just from the thought . . . I haven't read every page of the Bible. Chances are, I struggle with all the same things you do. I'm a pretty normal dude. I don't want you to think that my testimony is a result of me somehow being special or different than anyone else.

God talks to and guides anyone who will make the effort to listen. The choice to follow Him is your own; the very essence of real love. If God can do in the pages that follow, amazing things with my everyday life, what more will He do with yours?

Falling down

The story of the prodigal son, as told by Jesus in Luke 15:11-32, was once my theme song. I grew up reluctantly attending a stuffy Baptist church where my parents shoved me into a Sunday school class a couple times a month. It wasn't like I arrived kicking and screaming, but I much preferred mornings that involved sleeping in.

At the age of 14, my mother began to talk to me about baptism. So naturally, I got baptized. Again, it wasn't like I didn't want to. I believed that Jesus was the son of God, but honestly, I only got dunked because my momma told me to.

Later on, our family faced problems at this church – the kind of problems that lead many to hate Christians, walk away from the church and turn their back on God. After defaulting on the faith for a period, we found a smaller Baptist church close to the crib. There I was forced to play in the church band as a rebellious high schooler. At this point, the ways of the world controlled my every step. I did my best to be cool, fit in and talk the talk. I was enchanted by the lies of sex, drugs and hip hop. The last thing I wanted at that time in my life was to hear what a bad person I was every Sunday morning.

The final straw in my losing my faith came the summer between high school and college. One afternoon, I got a call saying a mutual friend had been shot point blank in the back of the head. Later that night on the news, I watched in horror as two of my friend's names flashed across the screen. D died two days later on July 3rd, 2004. The anger I felt at God afterward put me on a path towards my own destruction. I willingly plunged deep into the trap that so many people thrust themselves in. If God is good and all powerful, how can such tragedies occur?

College didn't help the situation. There I learned to fill the void in my soul with partying and dangerously aggressive behaviors. I tricked myself into believing that if I could just get more and more of that lifestyle, I'd be satisfied. But for many years, no satisfaction came my way. I drifted in and out of depressive thoughts, though I did my best to keep up a shiny outward appearance. During my freshman year of college, I actually told people that God didn't exist because of what happened to my friend. If He did exist, I'd rant, He was far too cruel to be who they say He is.

Getting Back Up

The amazing thing in all of this is that God never once left me. He only pursued me harder. He left His other 99 sheep just to come get me (Matthew 18:12-14), even though it took almost 7 years! The first thing God did was to show me it was true that He had never left my side and that He is alive and strong within all of us.

July 3rd, 2005, one year to the day, three carloads of D's friends from the local music shop where he was murdered descended upon his grave to pay our respects. I had never dealt with something this heavy before. Neither had anyone else that was there that day. I mostly remember that we were all so quiet, so speechless, so stunned and angry. We just stood there for 15 minutes or so in complete silence before someone gathered up the courage to say a few words. Suddenly D's father arrived, bawling just as hard as he had been at the funeral reception (which was also the first time I stepped foot in Southland Christian Church, but I'm getting ahead of myself). If I felt hurt and abandoned by almighty God, I couldn't imagine what D's pops was feeling that afternoon.

We slowly made our way back to the cars we'd left alongside the nearby path through the cemetery. It was an absolutely scorching hot July day in Lexington, Kentucky. It was enough to make me angry at how beautifully clear it was, when inside we were all clouded by so many questions. I remember specifically that there wasn't a single cloud in the sky.

As I neared my friend's car, that of the other guy who was shot but survived, he walked over to me and started crying. Right in the middle of our pain stricken embrace, teardrops began to fall from the heavens. I couldn't see any clouds in the sky, but nevertheless, there we stood in a gentle summer rain.

It was in that moment that I realized God hadn't left us. In fact, He was right there with us all along, mourning D's tragic death. I truly believe, the rain that fell at that moment was Jesus crying with us. After studying the Bible, I see that this moment is quite similar to what transpired in John 11:32-36, when Jesus wept over Lazarus' death. He was speaking to us, and for the first time, I heard His voice. On that day, I began to believe in God again.

Trying Times

Unfortunately, the miracle rain God sent us that day didn't lead me into a new amazing spiritual life. If anything, I just continued to stumble down the same path I had chosen for myself, thinking I knew best. I had seen how God is real and present in our everyday lives, but I still thought I was strong enough to do it all on my own. This, amigos, is not the case.

Fast forward five years. I graduated college, began a full time job in Lexington, quit that job, moved to New York to be an audio engineer, came home after five defeating months and found myself in the middle of the one of the worst economic crises' since the Great Depression. I was going from job to job, finding a new one, only to hate it and look for something else. The one thing I was holding onto in that tough time wasn't God, but a girlfriend.

I was crazy about her. She was passionate and driven. I thought we were going to change the world together. As soon as she graduated physician assistant school, I was going to pop the question. She called me her "rock" throughout two years of P.A. school. I served her selflessly as one should do for their wife or girlfriend, but it just wasn't enough. She distanced herself from me, instead of just breaking it off, making it harder in the end. With only a month to go before I planned to ask her to marry me, we suddenly broke up. I was sure it was just a break to get our future back on track, but only a couple weeks later, she was dating someone else.

Devastation ensued in my life. Darkness swallowed me whole. All I had clung to for two years was gone. I felt like I couldn't go on without her. How could this happen to me? *We were supposed to be together, God! How could You let this happen?*

At the time, I had just begun a new job working for my father. It was all I could find in the aftermath of the recession. It certainly wasn't my ideal job, nor was it even in my own city. It was an hour each way to get to the little backwards town where I was working. I'd wake up at 5 am and get home around 7 pm most days. It wasn't something I had a passion for. I would arrive home depleted, without any zest for life. Besides, I was convinced that I had nothing left to live for anyways. Entire weekends passed without getting out of bed or eating. I cried sporadically, almost every single day. My initial reaction was to return to my college ways. This only caused me more pain and I began to have very dark thoughts. I isolated myself more and more as negativity poured from my mouth. I couldn't make it more than a couple of minutes without thinking about how *my* future plans were ruined. I allowed something that now seems so insignificant to ruin an entire six month span of my life, starting that April.

To make matters worse, my brother was going through a similar situation. It was his first breakup. He was having a really hard time dealing with the horrible betrayal. Somehow he seemed worse off than I was. All this was taking a toll on my parents, especially my mother who was the only one there to comfort us. It was a dark summer, infected by depression that not only affected my life, but my family's as well. The whole time I wondered why God had again left me . . .

Changing My Tune

While eating at my favorite Mexican restaurant shortly after the breakup and chatting with the manager there, I was offered a gig for my "band" to play at the restaurant's biggest event of the year - Cinco de Mayo. I say "band" because we hadn't done much more at that point than jam every now and then. At the time, it was a great escape from my breakup. It was also how I was planning to get my girlfriend back.

In the weeks leading up to the show, I poured myself into preparing the set, organizing the event and practicing the songs. I didn't choose to rely on God at this point, but on myself, to play an awesome show and either win back my ex or meet someone new. Those weeks were also filled with one of the wettest springs on record in central Kentucky. I was so fearful that the outdoor show would get rained out, but I prayed, "God, if it is Your will, let there be sunshine on Cinco de Mayo."

The 5th of May rolled around. Not only was it the most beautiful day, but it was hot too. The kind of day where you wanted to sit on the porch at your favorite Mexican restaurant, eat chips and salsa and listen to live music. It was literally the first day without rain in weeks! Little did I know that despite my own intentions, God had set this day up as the beginning of a domino effect to bring me into a better life.

We played the show that afternoon and it went well, except for the fact that my ex didn't show up despite my extended invitation. That night, I proceeded to get highly intoxicated, though it didn't help in the least. I woke up the next day not only wanting to vomit, but with an overwhelming emptiness.

I had failed my mission to win back my ex and now I had no concert to distract me from my sorrows. Most of my high school and college friends had moved out of Lexington by then. Home suddenly felt like some unknown foreign city. My depression grew to be a dangerous mind game that all but drowned me.

An Afternoon in the Chapel

One afternoon in particular, on the way home from work, I became so upset I could barely drive straight. I couldn't even see I was crying so hard. As I did every day, I passed by Southland Christian Church on the way into town. This day was different. Something propelled me to pull into the parking lot and seek sanctuary.

I wearily wandered into the chapel to find 20 some kids practicing for their piano recitals. I took a seat where I thought I could best hide. I was hoping that someone from the church would be there to talk to, but no one paid me any attention. I felt just as alone as always. I kept wishing that some kind of minister type would walk up to me so I could unload this great burden onto them, but eventually the practice was over and I was the only human being that remained.

I fought back the tears until the kids left. Then they poured out like a salty waterfall. I snotted all over my shirt. I was a hot mess as they say. I picked up a Bible and thought, *God, I need You to speak to me.* I turned to a random passage, but it didn't seem relevant to the moment. Again I begged God to speak to me. Again I turned to a random passage. This time His word spoke directly to my soul!

You see, God talks to us in a way that can easily be overlooked. You can often think that it's just a funny coincidence and go on about your day. I believe that He does this so that only those who walk by faith in Him will find a better life. Faith is hard, no one questions that! Faith is pure though, and when you believe, suddenly you see God speaking to you in all matters of life.

The second time around I had turned to the book of Psalms. The first thing I read was, "Search me, O God, and know my heart; test me and know my anxious thoughts." (Psalm 139:23 NIV) It finally dawned on me that all this hurt and pain, all my searching for personal satisfaction, all the stumbling around on my own, was a direct result of not following Him. I knew in my heart that I wasn't living the way Jesus showed us to. Right then and there, for the first time in my life, I prayed a truly honest prayer for God to begin a new life in me. It was in that moment that my Old Testament ended and my New Testament, a life with Christ front and center as my Lord and Savior, began. Nothing would ever be the same!

Looking back, I think God wanted me to be alone with Him in that sanctuary. My whole life I had spent trying to do things on my own, and if *I* couldn't do it, I was putting my faith in someone or something else to do it for me. In that unforgettable afternoon He showed me that I had to trust in Him alone. I had to first and foremost have a relationship with Him, placing that above all other things.

Serve, Don't Wait Around to Be Served

I wish I could tell you that all my troubles just went away after giving myself up to Jesus, but this was actually just the first step in a long journey. I was still battling depression. However, I made changes in my life that began to lead me to a new path. I quit drinking all together. I read the Bible almost everyday. I listened to the entire Bible two times that summer with a recorded version that my mother had lent me. I went to church every Sunday, sometimes twice at different churches. I began to quit posting things on social media about partying and started putting up Bible verses. I started going to a Thursday night Bible study. Yet despite walking the walk, I was still struggling.

As I was preparing to go to the Thursday night Bible study for the first time after work, I put on a nice shirt in hopes to impress. Then as I was walking out, I was propelled for some reason to change my shirt and put on a more comfortable and humble soccer jersey. When I walked in to the house where the class was held, it was just as I had worried. I sat down and though people were talking all around me, I wasn't really a part of anybody's conversation. I felt alone again and was contemplating leaving.

Suddenly, a guy about my age named Jus told me he liked my Spain jersey. We got into a conversation about travel and it turned out that he was recently back from mission work in Mexico. As we formed a friendship over the next several weeks, I kept thinking that maybe God had crossed our paths so that Jus could somehow help me. What I now realize is that I needed to learn a lesson in selflessness, and my new friend was going to help me accomplish this.

Jus was really anxious to get back to Mexico. The only problem was that to support himself and the mission for the next year, he needed to raise around $16,000. That was just the bare minimum for him to get down there and back, live and do ministry for a year. When he first told me about his fund raising efforts, he was really skeptical. It wasn't going well and he was losing faith that he would make it back to Mexico. I started to think a lot about this.

Not surprisingly, God led our Bible study teacher to speak on sacrificial giving one night. Sure it sounded great, but when it comes to money, most people don't really have much left over to give. If they do, the last thing they are thinking about is giving it away. I decided I would give some money to Jus. Maybe $30 or something. It would barely make a dent, but then I could feel good about what I did.

One afternoon I went online to his personal site that was set up through the mission for him to fund raise to get back to Mexico and spread the gospel. The cost to donate 10% of what he needed grabbed my attention. Something within moved me to quit thinking about my self and start trusting in God. I made a 10% donation to the fund. What was quite interesting was that right after I hit send to complete the transaction, nothing special happened. I guess I thought an angel was going to appear and tell me that I had saved the world or something. I went about my day as usually and didn't feel much better or worse for what I had done.

The next Thursday at Bible study, Jus walked up to me and wouldn't stop thanking me. I felt embarrassed. He insisted that he must do something for me. I just wanted him to stop talking about it so I said, "Go to Mexico and spread the word then!" He agreed. He went on to tell me that he saw an email about the donation on his phone while driving and almost crashed out of shock. That day he had worked a fund raiser event that hadn't helped as much as he had hoped. He was all but ready to give up, when he saw that someone had just donated 10% of what he needed. He was suddenly recharged and with a renewed passion and faith in God, he reached his goal and flew back down to Mexico just a few months later.

God taught me an amazing lesson through my interactions with Jus. It changed my life. I realized that life isn't about me, me, me. It's about finding those who you can help and then sacrificially giving and serving them to the point where the only way you can follow through is to put your faith wholly in God. Otherwise, it would seem way too crazy and out of control. This was a huge way that God showed me *He* was in control and that I had to put my faith in Him. Once I took that leap of faith, things gradually started looking up!

MCL Woes

At this point it was July, and I felt as though things were starting to turn around. I wasn't fully healed by any means, but I had at least begun to force myself to get back to a normal life. With God at my side, I knew it was possible. However, my main mistake was that I was still trying to do it by my own power instead of His. I hadn't yet 100% given into the life that God had planned for me. I tried to fill my time up with numerous activities to stay busy and not think about the breakup, or my brother's similar situation, or the fact that I hated my job or the fact that I was single and alone. I started playing in different sports leagues. I was still seeking a satisfaction in my own glory from scoring goals or winning games, instead of seeking God's perfect will and humbling myself to serve in that way.

God is sovereign. This means that He is completely in control of good *and* evil. He doesn't inflict evil on us, but He allows it to happen for our greater good and His glory. Very early into the summer soccer season (actually *the first game*) I kicked the ball at the same time as a much bigger and stronger opponent. The result, I found out the next morning in the ER, was that I had partially torn my MCL. I couldn't walk for almost a month without crutches. I couldn't get surgery since the tear was partial, so I had to just sit on the couch and let it heal naturally.

All the things that I had been trying to fill my life with before were no longer an option - sports, my band, exercising. Just when I thought I was peeking my head out of the tunnel of depression, I was suddenly thrown right back into its dark abyss. This time it was almost worse, because I couldn't physically move around. Having been so close to breaking free, it was like being kicked while I was down.

This was God rebuking me again. He knew He was so close to having me back that He had to keep me from my old habits. I believe He allowed me to tear the ligament in my knee, so I would understand that He is all powerful, in control and has a much better plan for my life than the things I would choose to fill it with. "Many are the plans in the mind of a man, but it is the purpose of the LORD that will stand." (Proverbs 19:21 ESV) I had to remember to put all my faith, efforts and energy into my relationship with the one true King.

Testify

One Sunday at a small Hispanic church that I occasionally attended, they had asked if anyone wanted to share a testimony or an encouraging word. Without being prepared, I cowered out of doing it. After some thought, I decided to show up prepared the next week, although they didn't ask, so I didn't share. But guess who showed up that week without having ever told me prior that he knew of this small church? I walked into the tiny sanctuary that day to find Jus sitting there. After service he shared with me that he had almost reached his goal in fundraising to get back to Mexico. I felt encouraged and could see that God was already making huge changes in our lives. I decided I would come back the next week and give my testimony for sure.

I arranged with Chal, the pastor, to give my testimony, that way it was set up in advance. I practiced it over and over again since giving a testimony in Spanish would be harder than in my native tongue. Not to mention, I had never gotten up in front of a church to speak before. Nor had I ever bared it all in front of others with a personal testimony. I was pretty nervous on the car ride over to the church and when I arrived I only got more nervous. I barely even noticed that there was another gringa in the congregation that afternoon. I was usually the only non-Hispanic person besides the pastor and his family.

When NBC reporters asked Olympic gymnast Gabby Douglas how she kept her composure in the 2012 London Summer games, she answered that she meditated on Scripture. Many people were probably thinking, *Why would that help?* I was thinking, *I feel you Gabs!* I just started meditating on God's goodness and asked Him to give me strength not to butcher my testimony. I also asked that He would put the words on my tongue, as He says He will do in Luke 12:11-12. Finally, it came time to give my testimony.

I walked up and felt an overwhelming calm that had not been with me since I had nervously gotten out of the car. I delivered my testimony and wasn't nervous at all, as His power guided me. I felt stronger with each word I professed. As I walked back to my seat, it felt like the ten million pounds that had gathered upon my shoulders that summer were suddenly lifted off. I breathed deep and actually smiled. I think it was literally the first smile I had cracked in months.

When we share God's love with others and profess His love, His blessings pour out. As Gabby also said, "The glory goes up to Him, and the blessings fall down on me!" I finally saw that life's purpose is having a relationship with God and helping as many lost brothers and sisters find that same thing, so that they can unload a million pounds off their shoulders too.

Answered Questions

I had constantly and quite angrily questioned God that summer about why He had ripped me from the girl that I loved. I believed then and still believe now, that it was God who separated us. He didn't do it to be mean, but He did body slam me so that I would quit putting my faith in a girl and start putting it in Him. If it meant putting me through a summer of Hell on earth, then that was a tiny price to pay.

What Hell on earth are you facing right now? I can confidently tell you that it is just a small toll to pay on your journey to know the Father. Turn your life over to Him now and watch the healing begin!

One of the questions that I asked most often is, "Why would You take her from me?" I was truly convinced she was my soul mate. Don't think I've always gotten this out of shape over a break up. I was halfway down on bended knee when she left me. In this pain I thought, *God, there is no other girl like her. I'll never be able to find someone the same!* I just couldn't see there being anyone else.

I don't know if you know this, but God is a mad funny Dude. He answered my question, but again, without physically speaking to me. He showed me through a chance meeting with a girl that I thought couldn't exist.

The gringa that had showed up to the Hispanic church the day I gave my testimony, turned out to be the answer to that question. We got to talking after the service and found that we had a lot in common. She had lived in Spain like me and several other countries as well. We exchanged work emails. She gave me her business card. When I got home I looked at it and was shocked. She had the same last name as my ex and a very similar first name that rhymed. She was a cute blonde, like my ex. They both spoke Spanish and wanted to change the world. She was a loving person that cared about the under served populations of the world. After a few "dates" which were really just casual hang outs, we found ourselves attracted to each other.

When I finally found out where her apartment was, I was dumbfounded. She lived right across the street from a small church that I had recently been to. In fact, going to a service at that church was the last thing my ex and I had done before she pushed me away forever.

God not only answered my question with, "Yes, there are other girls out there like your ex," but He did so with stunning similarities; and in my own medium sized city of Lexington! The gringa and I never officially dated, because God had other plans

25

for our lives. But I know that He crossed our paths at that moment in time to bring us out of the depression we were both facing from previous breakups.

Southern Boy Goes South

As God continued to blow my mind left and right with revelations of a new life through Him, I thought about giving it all up to go serve somewhere. Because of my Spanish speaking capabilities, I really wanted to go to a Latin American country and use the gifts God gave me to serve there. It was difficult to pick a place to go. I started thinking about South America and some of the countries down there. I was having a hard time narrowing it down. Peru sounded great and I was thinking about going there to teach English.

I also remembered seeing this tourist video about Chile in Spanish class in college. Ever since then I was quite intrigued, yet really knew nothing about the country. After studying in Spain in 2008, I got on the website of the program I went with and found out that they had service learning programs as well. They had programs in Chile, Peru, Argentina and Brazil. Brazil was eliminated first because I didn't speak Portuguese and wanted to use my Spanish. Not knowing much about Chile, I leaned towards Peru and then Argentina. Keep in mind however, that this seemed at first more like an insane idea I had, rather than something I was actually going to do.

One Thursday that summer, I took a much needed personal day from work to take care of some things I couldn't ever get done on the weekend like dentist appointments and job searching. I made it a point that afternoon to drop by the study abroad office at the University of Kentucky to stick my face and résumé in front of someone and beg for a job. As with most bureaucratic university types, I was brushed aside and told to wait in the hallway. Maybe someone would talk to me later when they could break away from their busy schedule. I waited in the hall for a while. Fortunately, that was how God had planned it!

While I was sitting there feeling unwanted, a college student that worked in the office walked by. I had never met him before, but he looked at me as he passed and said, "Great show the other day, Mateo!" as if we knew each other. I was pretty taken back. I thought that no good had come from the Cinco de Mayo show. Come to find out, he had been there. His compliment really gave me a boost amidst my moments of extreme doubt. He returned to his office and I was thinking that was that.

I waited so long that the student actually came back out to leave and we struck up a conversation. It turned out he was an alumni of the same study abroad program as me. I told him I had studied in Spain and that I had a crazy idea to go abroad again and teach

English. Just as I was about to tell him that Peru or Argentina sounded good, he told me that he had just gotten back from studying in Valparaíso, Chile and that it had changed his life much like studying in Spain had done for me.

Looking back at that dark summer now, I can see a set path that God placed me on. I could have easily blown off much of it to coincidence, but it was far too powerful and convicting to be coincidence. There were too many answered prayers and blessings at exactly the right moment for me to say that it was anything less than the majestic guidance of the Lord! It all just fell into place like it was supposed to.

I took this well timed encounter as God nudging me towards Chile. I had no idea what was down there, what I would do, who I would meet or what Chile was like, but I threw all that on God's mighty shoulders and submitted to His will for me. After all, it isn't God's style to use someone nearby to change you. He would rather send a foreigner to a strange land to do His great works like in the book of Jonah.

Through the Fog

The last week of August, I was told I was being let go of my job. This wasn't really a huge source of disappointment, because I couldn't say that I really loved that job, but I wasn't sure what I would do. I had applied to be a volunteer English teacher in Chile and would be leaving late September, so I needed every dollar I could save until then to support the cause.

As I often did, I prayed, cried and talked to God in my early morning drives to work. Watching the sunrise over His creation will never leave you unsatisfied. Many morning as the sun came over the beautiful horse farms of central Kentucky, I would cross over the Kentucky River. There was often a lot of fog in that area that early in the morning. Sometimes it was so heavy I was completely surrounded and couldn't see anything else. Other days, for no particular reason, it was less or not there at all.

I read in the Old Testament that God would appear as smoke or fog to the Jews as they made their exodus from Egypt to the Promised Land in Israel. (Deuteronomy). Sometimes God would descend on the Israelite camp as fog and not move for a long time. This was a command to the Israelites that they were to stay put until the Holy fog had lifted, signifying it was time to once again pick up all they had and leave.

Those mornings, I was reminded that God is always with us through the Holy Spirit as I would enter into the fog. It was no surprise to me at all, that after seeing fog almost every morning that summer on the way to work, I saw nothing but a bright and sunny valley on my last day. God was showing me that His plan was in full effect and that it was time to move on!

La Gringa

The last week before departing to Chile, I finally confronted the gringa with my feelings for her. Though we seemed to be falling for each other, she recognized that it was not wise for us to jump into a relationship with me going abroad. I was blinded by my need to not be alone and of course by her pretty smile. As we shared a goodbye hug, the last thing she left me with was the gift of freedom on my way to Chile.

"Whatever you find or whatever God has planned for you down in Chile, I won't stand in the way of that," she stated. I was a little upset, but it was truly a great gift and would prove to be very important in the future. God taught me through her that we sometimes must leave all that we know and love to follow Him.

I was so thankful for the healing that this friendship brought me and for her selfless gift to set me free to serve, explore, live and love in Chile. With a heavy heart, we said goodbye for what would be forever. The next day I flew to Chile to see what God had in store for me!

Los Andes

Anyone that has ever flown anywhere, let alone internationally to Latin America, knows that delays and cancellations are *mandatory*! I made it to Dallas from Lexington just fine, but at 10:30 pm that night, our 9:00 pm flight to Santiago was cancelled. This meant that I was going to miss my free transport from Santiago to Valparaíso, which was going to cost me $120 dollars that I didn't really have to throw around for a private pickup. Though Jesus taught us not to worry (Matthew 6:27-30), we still can't seem to fully give in to the notion. With that and the fact that I had to spend the night in Dallas and get up after two hours of sleep for a 9 hour flight, I was more than a little frustrated. Didn't I know that God was in control, planning every detail?

The next day we flew out early that morning. On the plane was an entire ski school from Vermont, taking their fall break to train in the Andes. I sat by a young girl that was an instructor. We chatted on and off for the duration of the flight. Later on, I pulled out my Bible. Somehow we started talking about it, I think since it was a Spanish/English Bible. It was one of the first times I got to tell someone what the most important thing in their life will ever be. I showed her my bookmark which had John 3:16 written on it and told her that she could read the whole Bible, but this was really the one line that mattered most.

Nothing came of it right then and there. She said something like, "That's not really for me right now . . ." There was no Vermont revival, no baptism in the bathroom sink. The stewards didn't sing a hymn and she never got close to making a confession of faith, but a seed was planted that day. Who knows what God did with that? All we can do is pray that she will one day know the Father's love.

I was very thankful that I even got the chance to fail at telling someone about Jesus. As He says, "Whoever acknowledges me before others, I will also acknowledge before my Father in heaven." (Matthew 10:32 NIV)

As we descended into Santiago, God had yet another trick up His sleeve. It was nearing twilight. I just so happened to be sitting on the correct side of the plane to be able to see a gorgeous red sunset pouring through the amazing Andes mountains. God sends us these gifts of beauty from time to time to remind us of His incredible power and creation. Nothing like a 10 hour delay in Dallas to eventually put you in awe of the Maker!

La Porteña

I was picked up at the airport in Santiago by a Chilean *colectivo* (shared cab) driver named Esteban. As we sped though the Cordillera de la Costa (coastal mountain range) that sits between Santiago and Valparaíso and Viña del Mar, we got to talking. I found out that he was a believer and we talked about some Christian bands that we liked. He even gave me his contact info and invited me to his church. I was thinking that things in Chile were already shaping up nicely. Yet one of the biggest mysteries was about to be unveiled - my host family.

Of course I was nervous to meet the family I would be living with for the next several months. As we pulled into Valpo, we quickly exited for Viña, where my host family lived. With each turn we rode higher and higher into *los cerros* (neighborhood hills). My anticipation heightened and a nervous cramp formed in my side. We finally arrived to Calle

Madre de Dios (literally Mother of God Street), which was quite a fitting name. Funny how that would happen! I was feeling completely out of my element. Before I even had my backpack out of the car, Juan Carlos, my host father, greeted me with a warm smile. We walked across a small bridge that connected the apartment complex with the street and entered the gate. When we got down to their floor, Juan Carlos waved me on to enter first. I knocked on the door with anxious nerves jittering throughout me.

At this point, time somehow momentarily stopped. The next few seconds were more of a beautiful dream than real life interaction. The door opened slowly and . . . Pause! I should really throw in some more background info before I go on. Prepare to intensify your suspense!

A week or so before leaving for Chile, I get a call from a girl named Tanya who worked for the program. She wanted to know if I would be willing to live with a family that had cats, even though I put on my housing form that I'm somewhat allergic to them. I didn't want to be picky or difficult, so I told her to place me as best they could with what I wrote, though I'm definitely not a cat person. She answered that she would do what she could. As it turns out, I ended up getting moved to the family in Viña as a second option. I was originally going to live with a family in Valpo, but once again, God's plans are bigger than anything that we try to make. I know we are supposed to love everyone like in Mark 12:31 (I suppose that includes God's creatures too?), but my dislike of cats would change my life forever.

I was told beforehand that I had a host sister that was younger than me. I thought it would be fun to have a host sister since I've never had a real sister before. I won't lie. I must confess, since God already knew my thoughts, that I had wondered if she would be pretty or fun to hang out with. I wondered if we'd become friends or if she would just write me off as another American dude that her family was hosting for a few months. After ciphering through those thoughts, I pretty much decided that I shouldn't be thinking like that and it would never be in God's plan for my host sister to be beautiful or to be anything other than a friend and sister in Christ. But how many times can I relearn that I don't have a clue what God's plan is? I can only listen as He speaks to me through life's crazy path. So where were we? Ah yes . . .

The door opens. I'm almost knocked off my feet by what stood before me. A smile beamed up at me, shining like a fabulous sunset over Valparaíso and singing with a sweet voice in a soft greeting, "Hola!" Long gorgeous jet black hair twisted and flowed over her shoulders, all the way down to her waist. Round cheeks with innocent dimples accentuated her radiant smile. She batted her green eyes nervously, each one in sync with my resounding heartbeats. She was tall for a Latina, meaning she was still shorter than me, but pleasantly, we saw eye to eye as a man and woman might when they lock gazes upon initial divine encounter. This angelic being stood before me, glowing as if her heart and spirit was as pure and beautiful as her outer self. I might have momentarily gone to Heaven and back. It's impossible to tell in moments like these!

Suddenly, I was snapped back into reality. I was in South America for the first time and had just arrived at my host family's door step. Time sped back to its eternal pace and I was suddenly horrified that I might have just spent the last three hours starring at my host sister! My knowledge of Hispanic culture kicked in and I rushed in for a kiss to avoid what I was worried was an already awkward greeting. I placed my cheek against hers, as is the custom and gave a hello kiss. Her skin was soft and her energy was warm. I was in shock!

Quickly, I greeted my host brother and gave my host mother a full embrace. I was ecstatic to begin discovering this new path God had opened! Over the next hour, I learned what a deeply loving and close family I had just entered into. They were always laughing and spending time together. It was absolutely, positively infectious. All the anxieties that had built up during my arrival, quickly melted away and I settled into my new life in Chile. I was so thankful to the Father for the journey He had sent me on that summer and that was still just the opening act.

Answered Prayer

I began volunteering at a local NGO - Acción Emprendedora in Valpo. I taught English class to entrepreneurs who had their own businesses and wanted to be able to converse with foreigners to increase sales. I also taught a web design class that showed them how to create and market a website for free, via social media and Wordpress. When I wasn't teaching, I helped out as best I could in the office. Sometimes I'd go with the director to recruit more students in Valpo and Viña. I also worked with a lady named Mariela.

I decided it was time to drop all my depressive ways and thoughts from the summer and start again fresh. God had brought me a new beginning and it was time to rejoice in the joy (Psalm 30:5) that was now in my life. I went back to being me: a little wild, very lighthearted and plenty easy going. Mariela didn't initially know what to think of *me*, the spontaneous gringo. As I spent more and more time around her, I won her friendship over to the point where she opened up to me about her marriage, her ex and her relationship with God.

One Friday I got to work and it was just Mariela there. I could tell something bothered her. She told me her friend was very sick, to the point of being in the hospital with not much hope. I didn't know what to do other than ask God for help. I suggested that we pray. Mariela was a little weirded out that we would do something like that at work, but she gave in. We just thanked God for His goodness and asked that He heal Mariela's friend.

We know that by faith, Christ is the great healer (Mark 5:34). When I came in that next Monday, Mariela was so excited to see me. She grabbed me by the shoulders as soon as I entered and told me that her friend's health had miraculously turned around. She said, "God answered our prayers!" After the summer I'd been through, I knew that God hears us and answers our prayers by faithfulness. I was so filled with the joy of the Spirit, that it was hard to concentrate. Still, I wasn't as surprised as Mariela by the outcome, because I had already seen how He is faithful to those who come to Him in prayer.

Sometimes I wonder if God sent me all the way to South America, just to pray with Mariela that day and encourage her faith. It's not like I started a new church or baptized new brothers and sisters in Christ during my time in Chile. I tried to be servant minded and give my time and efforts to the best of my ability. I hope and pray that some of the seeds planted that trip did not fall along the path (Luke 8:5), but hit the good soil. The truth is, I will never understand God's plan for me while I'm just His servant here on Earth. All we can do is try to interpret the guidance He gives when He talks to us through people, signs and chance encounters.

Chilean Church

Remember Jus? When he found out I was going to Chile, he put me in contact with a guy he knew that had done mission work down there. He suggested that I check out Union Church in Viña, since I was looking to find a new church home. I was initially very excited to do so until Esteban invited me to his church. I was confused with the mixed signals, so I decided to try Esteban's church in Valpo first, since I seemed to be hot on God's path.

I went the second Sunday I was in Chile with my host mother and sister. They are Catholic and it was the very first time in their lives that they had gone to a Christian church of another denomination. Esteban humbly withheld from me during the ride from Santiago that he just so happened to be the worship band leader. The worship music began that morning and I was feeling like I was in the right place.

43

11 songs, an hour of church updates and an angry sermon later, I never wanted to come back. My host family was horrified. Now I don't wish to speak poorly of my brothers and sisters in Christ. However, I find it hard to believe that a church where many cannot help but charismatically dance their way up to the front in obvious attempts to be seen by everyone else, truly do so because the Spirit is so alive within them. Jesus warned us of the ways of the Pharisees in Matthew 6:1-4.

When the preacher made everyone raise their Bible in the air so he could publicly shame those who didn't bring one, I decided I'd check out Union Church the following Sunday. Jesus warned us against false prophets and teachers too (Matthew 7:15-20), because He knew how abundant they would be one day. I think He sent me to that church to learn what an unhealthy church body looks like. God sure had a lot of lessons for me to learn that summer!

The next Sunday, I went to Union Church. Though it resembled a mixture of a Catholic and Baptist church from its outward appearance, it had an internationally non-denominational congregation. As the first service I attended began, I felt right at home. I wanted desperately to be a part of the church, to serve and to maybe even play in the church band. If it was hard for me to break into a church home back in Kentucky, it felt like an unmovable mountain blocking my way here in Chile. Yet, Jesus told us, "Truly I tell you, if you have faith as small as a mustard seed, you can say to this mountain, 'Move from here to there,' and it will move. Nothing will be impossible for you." (Matthew 17:20 NIV)

After singing a few worship songs, pastor Waldo encouraged spiritually strong members of the church to find someone to pray for. In that moment I locked eyes with what looked like a middle aged gringa and then immediately looked away. She paused and started to make her way back to her seat, coming from the special prayer up front. Then as if prompted by the Holy Spirit, she came over to pray for me. I was a little scared and didn't even initially understand that she was speaking English to me. Her name was Rose Marie. She was of Canadian descent, but had been living in Chile and Bolivia for over 20 years.

"I was going to go back to my seat, but then the Spirit moved me to come talk to you," she whispered, as the music played on. I immediately became fully overwhelmed with the journey I had been on to arrive at that point, the goodness of God and the pain that I was still more or less running from in my mind. I began sobbing. Rose just hugged me tight and loved and prayed for me with the voice and intuition of a mother. I knew that this is where God wanted me to land at that very moment. I love how He talks to us!

After the service, Rose introduced me to the pastor and told him that I was interested in playing in the band. He loved the idea and introduced me to the band and Alejandro, the worship leader. They invited me to come to the next practice a few days later. For the rest of my time in Chile, I served as a bass player and drummer in the worship band. I made a bunch of Chilean and foreign friends, felt wanted by the culture and right with God's kingdom in Chile. Never had His path and voice been clearer!

La Campana

So you're probably wondering what happened with my host sister? Haha! Well Fernanda, better known as Feña and I became best friends. She was initially shy around me and I was scared to talk to her. Then her mother suggested she show me where the ATM was in the main plaza of the neighborhood we lived in. After that, we did everything together.

Our favorite thing to do was watch the stunning sunsets as God turned off the lights each day in Chile. Turns out, the university she went to was right across the street from where I worked in Valpo. How perfectly designed, like someone upstairs came up with this! When I got off work and she got out of class, we would meet up and hop a *micro* (mini-bus) for Viña, las Salinas, Reñaca, Concón and any other magnificent sunset lookout we could find along the coast.

Now there is nothing more romantic than watching the most colorful and vibrant sunsets you can imagine on the beach with a beautiful Chilean girl! Early on I wanted to pursue Feña as a girlfriend, but I was determined to do the right thing in the eyes of the Lord and not to break the rules or trust of my host family. After confiding in Mariela, she finally told me that we were just wasting precious time. That's when I got it in my head to make a move. I kept putting it off though, because I was hoping for guidance from up above.

That ended up being very healthy for us. My friendship with Feña grew and we had deep talks about God and what we are doing here on this rock for a whisper of moment. I was so attracted to the pureness of her soul, the goodness of her heart and yes, her pretty smile! Eventually while dining out one evening, a friend of hers made a comment in Spanish about how she liked someone. Feña told her to be quiet really quick, obviously feeling embarrassed and vulnerable. Fortunately for me, my Spanish had never been better and I understood exactly what was said. I was able to read into it that she liked me. Still, I wanted God to show us the perfect moment, if it were in His will for us to be together.

One weekend, we hopped on the *metro* (train) and headed out of town to Limache, towards the Andes. From there we took a micro to a small pueblo called Olmué. At the last stop, you can get off and hike up the mountain to a national park with several great hiking trails. The main trail is about 7 km and leads you all the way to the top of the highest mountain in the area named La Compana (The Bell).

We hiked about a third of the way up and went off into the forest to find a shady spot for our sac lunch. After eating, we found a nice cool spot to relax and enjoy the view, God's creation and each other's company.

It was in that moment, exactly one month after I opened the front door to be blown away, that I made my move. We had been sitting there for a while, nervously chatting about nothing. It was so obvious that we liked each other, but I was still waiting on that perfect moment. Suddenly a gentle breeze lightly rattled the trees for the first time since we had been there. Since I had learned that these occurrences can be the methods with which God talks to us, I knew it was time. I'm pretty sure He was saying, "Shalalalala, kiss the girl!" (Assuming God is a Little Mermaid fan). Never had I experienced such a romantic and pure first kiss. Doing things God's way is so rewarding!

A Bible for the Desert

Throughout my time in Chile, loose change began to amass in a pile on my desk. I used the *gamba* pieces (100 pesos) to pay for public transportation. Anything smaller got tossed in a jar. After 10 weeks, I had a decent cache of change. I figured that I would find a good use for it and with the way things had been going, God would point it out!

My second to last Sunday at Union church, they mentioned that they were going to take up a special collection to buy children's Bibles for an orphanage outside of San Pedro de Atacama. This is a popular spot to visit in the north of Chile. I didn't get a chance to go, but was excited by the opportunity to spread the gospel. They mentioned that one Bible would cost 5000 pesos or about ten bucks.

I got home that morning after the service and made a beeline for my jar. I wanted to see if my savings would cover the cost of a desert Bible. It was hard not to crack a smile and look upwards in wonder after counting up the change. The final sum was exactly 5000 pesos. As the most famous psalmist King David wrote, "The LORD is my Shepherd, I lack nothing." (Psalm 23:1 NIV)

A New Start

My time in Chile was over far too soon. There was an emotional goodbye as I left. Feña couldn't help but let the tears flow. I tried to stay strong, because I knew I would be all alone for the next month as I backpacked from Uruguay to Ecuador. I took off and spent most of the next month on a fantastic adventure through God's creation.

I had not exactly been the most Christ-like in neglecting to pay for the original taxi ride from Santiago. Tanya, the program representative for Chile in the States, had been emailing back and forth with me about the outstanding charge on my account. I admit I expressed some frustrations for being put in an expensive situation when I had not done anything to deserve it. But C'est la vie! Things happen! Roll with the punches!

Tanya didn't get upset, but very nicely and professionally explained to me how it had been the safest, quickest and best option at the time. She also mentioned that her company was hiring for a new Chile representative in Austin, TX. Now it was as if the annoying circumstance had become a part of His plan.

I found out about the job opening right before I left for my backpacking trip. Anyone who has spent a few weeks in South American hostels knows that internet access is spotty at best. I explained to Tanya that I was very interested, but would be traveling for several weeks. On my second to last day in Ecuador, I spent almost an hour trying to upload my résumé in an email to Tanya at a shady internet café. I figured that since I wasn't able to apply online and had rushed out a résumé, I probably wouldn't stand a chance. God often has other things in mind.

Turns out, when I got back home to Kentucky, they wanted to interview me for the position via Skype. Never did I feel like I nailed an interview like I nailed that one! After a follow-up phone interview, I felt like this could possibly be a new beginning for me. As I prayed the whole time I was in South America, "Not my will be done, but Yours Father!"

The waiting game was driving me cray! Feña came to visit for a month in the U.S. and since I had no job and was checking my email every minute to see if they had decided yet, we took off for the northeast. Feña had never been outside of Chile. In five days we toured and visited friends in Philly, D.C. and NYC. It was a great distraction, but when we got home to Lextown, I was disappointed to find there was still nothing new on the issue.

One thing that I find interesting about my relationship with God, is that there are times when I need to wait on Him to figure out where I need to go. He will eventually talk to me in His infinitely creative ways and it will become as clear as the path before me. Other times, we are called to be proactive. Jesus said, "Ask and it will be given to you; seek and you will find; knock and the door will be opened to you." (Luke 11:9 NIV)

I felt like this was an amazing opportunity and I didn't want to let it get away. It felt like God had set me up with this chance as a new beginning, but now I had to make it happen. I emailed the staff in Chile and told them I had interviewed for the position. I had won them over while in Chile, and as fellow believers, they were happy to help. They sent a recommendation to the headquarters on my behalf. A few days later I checked my email after hopping out of the shower. To my excitement, there was a message asking me if I would accept the position.

Before I screamed, danced and ran all over the house half naked, I just thanked the Father for the fruits of the amazing journey He had taken me on. All things are possible through God! Here I was, broken and dangerously lost just months before. Now, through faith in God, I had a brand new start!

Port A Baptism

The next week, Feña and I drove to Austin, TX, about 17 hours away from Lexington. I found an apartment and got moved in. We had a couple days before my first day at work, so we took off for the Gulf to spend that time at the beach. The lady that helped me find an apartment had mentioned that Port Aransas was the closest beach from Austin.

Feña got really ill at this point. She couldn't eat much and spent the whole time resting and Skyping back to Chile for medical advice from her brother. When I wasn't taking care of her, I took a chance to enjoy the beach. She took a nap and I went for a long run up and down the coast. It was a good chance to process through all that had happened in 2011, since things had been happening so fast I could hardly keep up. The fact that I was running up and down this beach in Texas was proof that God had a plan for me all along. I just had to listen.

I remembered that Chal had offered to baptize me again before leaving for Chile, after hearing that my first baptism was more or less following orders. At the time, I had thought that was unnecessary. It's true, once you are saved by Christ's greatest gift of love and mercy, you can't undo it. Still, a reaffirmation of faith, especially one that was completely of my own will, would only serve as glory to God for His incredible plan.

Being late January in Port A, there wasn't anyone around and I would have felt weird asking a stranger to baptize me. I decided to let the Gulf do the work. I waded out into the salty waters. It was winter, but the water wasn't so cold that you couldn't get in. The tide had kicked up a little with the intensifying coastal breeze. I got far enough out that the water was up to my waist. At this point, I thought that there would be this miracle moment and I would know that it was time. Yet just like that day in the sanctuary, it was just me and God out there.

That's how our relationship with Him works. It can only be you and Him. When we put other things in-between that relationship like work, ambitions, sports, relationships, drugs, sex and any number of other idols, we distance ourselves from the love of the Father.

An overwhelming since of urgency came over me. I couldn't wait another second to proclaim my step of faith. I lunged backward and submerged myself into the Gulf. As I arose and wiped the salt water from my eyes, I saw a white bird shoot through the sky. It appeared to be flying out from . . . *me*. It just took off out to sea until I couldn't see it anymore.

It was a beautiful moment, because all the birds I had seen that day were flying along the coast. Not a single one had flown out to sea like that. I felt like a piece of my soul was going up to heaven to be prepared as a place with the Father, like Jesus promised us in John 14:2.

Mission Code Name: Chicken Nuggets

I started working in ATX for the same study abroad provider I'd previously volunteered with and loved it. Everyone was really friendly, young and had similar interests. Austin is a really cool and active city. I was immediately happy with my surroundings. Still, moving to a new city by yourself can be difficult. Feña went back to Chile to start a new semester and I settled into my new life.

I got a bike so I could explore my new city better. I would often go downtown and ride around. The one thing that absolutely gripped my heart every visit I made to the city center, was the fact that homelessness was rampant. One evening I saw a man passed out under a bench near the river. His few belongings were scattered around him. A bottle of rubbing alcohol was mostly empty next to his outstretched arm. By his breathing I could tell he was still alive. I thought, *I don't know how to help this man, but if I were him, I'd love to wake up and find a sandwich.* I sailed up to Jimmy Johns and got a Turkey Tom, my favorite, hopefully his too. I cruised back to the river and left the sandwich where he would see it when he woke. On it I wrote a small and simple message, but one I know to be true and infinitely powerful - "Jesus loves you!"

As I crossed the bridge that night to return to my cozy apartment on the Southside, I thought that getting the job was probably only an excuse to get me to Austin. What plans did the Father have for me here that related to expanding His kingdom of believers? I prayed to God that He would show me how to be His servant here in Austin and that He would melt my heart for the less fortunate. After that, I started periodically doing ministry where I would spread love and hope to the homeless community of Austin.

I found out, after a few nights of delivering sandwiches downtown, that there was a homeless shelter call ARCHES. A couple of times I made turkey or ham sandwiches and brought them down and handed them out. I was a little taken back by the response. Most people said they weren't hungry, the sandwich didn't look very good or could I buy them a cheeseburger? After being discouraged at my first few attempts, I thought, *What does everyone love to eat?* Duh - chicken nuggets!

One night I planned to swing by Chick-Fil-A and pick up a bunch of chicken nuggets to take down to ARCHES. Being new to the ATX, I searched online for a Chick-Fil-A and found one on UT's campus about 17 streets north of my delivery point. With God's goodness coursing through my veins, I blasted off for 24th street, which was *way* farther than I realized.

On the way, farther north than I had previously explored, I hopped onto the sidewalk because the street became a one-way. At a certain point, I slowed down as I passed what appeared to be homeless woman. I wanted to help her in some way, but had nothing to give her. I prayed, "Father, help me help this woman!" I tore off towards where I had pin pointed the Chick-Fil-A. If I could pick up the food fast enough, I could perhaps meet this woman on this road as I came back with some piping hot chicken nuggets.

Unfortunately, when I arrived, there was no Chick-Fil-A. Google had lied. There was also no restaurant nearby that sold anything similar. I began asking random UT students. They sent me on a wild goose chase around campus. Almost an hour later, I came to what appeared to be a cafeteria in the center of campus. They didn't have a Chick-Fil-A, but they did have a Wendy's. Their chicken nuggets are pretty good too. I ordered as many chicken nuggets as would fit in my backpack. This order took a while and the staff was very curious as to why I would order so many nuggets. I told them they were for some friends of mine.

Who should walk into that very Wendy's and ask for a cup of water, but that woman I had passed over an hour ago. I was no longer anywhere near the road where we had first crossed paths. God had answered my prayer! I asked her if she was hungry and ordered her a baked potato, which is all she wanted. We started talking. I didn't want to preach to her. I just wanted to let her know why I was doing this and who it was that could really change her life. I don't remember the exact words of the conversation, but it went something like this:

"Are you a student or something?" she asked.

"No, I'm just a crazy guy that likes chicken nuggets!" I joked.

"Well then why are you here?"

"I'm actually here because someone sent me."

She paused and stared deeply into my soul with weary eyes and said so confidently, so gently, "Yah . . . I know who sent you!"

I felt a shiver run down my spine. This whole deal where God talks to me in His crazy different ways just got too real! I was overwhelmed on the ride back downtown. I struggled to fight back tears and not get run over by the busy campus traffic.

Why do I tell you this? It is not to gain your praise, for I only seek the approval of my Father in Heaven. To one day hear, "Well done my good and faithful servant," is the longing of my heart. But I tell you these things, that by my testimony, you would know that God is alive and moving in all of us! How He desires a relationship with you! If you'll just listen, you will see Him working all around you, in everything you do. Would you make that crazy step of faith in Him today? What is holding you back? Do you *still* need to hear more stories of how I've heard Him talk to me? *Adelante!* (forward!)

Togolese Discipleship

Wouldn't you know I was dead on with my guess that chicken nuggets were universally approved! After being shut down with my ham samis, I got the warmest reception for bringing chicken nuggets! Just to see their smiles and hear their comments warmed my heart. One guy took a bite and with amazement and wonder in his voice said, "They hot out the *oven* too!" That night, I got the chance to talk to people, not just hand them something and move on. Again, I didn't preach to them, just gave them some nuggets in the name of Jesus and told them they are loved. As I handed out the last 5-pack, I reached the last person that had gathered outside of ARCHES that night. The amount of nuggets was perfectly enough!

The last man I talked to was off by himself. He remembered me from bringing down sandwiches before and said, "I thanked God for you!" Wow! To be recognized as God's servant was humbling. So was his story.

We started talking and I found out how he had landed in Austin. Enos Fepke came to the U.S. from Togo, where he was born in Africa. He was a chemist who specialized in making soft drinks with tropical flavors from West Africa. Some Russians had recruited him to make his drinks in the U.S. They brought him to Florida and then on to Texas. Once they got what they wanted from him, they robbed him of his few possessions and passport and left him for dead on the highway outside of Round Rock, just north of Austin. He'd found his way back to Austin and was now living on the sidewalk of 7th street, in the heart of downtown. The amazing thing is he didn't seem to harbor hate for those men or God for the events that had landed him as a homeless man in Texas, thousands of miles away from his native Togo.

Over the next several months, I would visit him on 7th street to bring food or clothes. I thought that it would be my mission to help him find his way, his new beginning. God was tugging on my heart to do something drastic. I fought it for months, but God is infinitely patient and everlastingly persistent. Jesus warned us in Matthew 25:45, that when we don't help one of our brothers in need on the street, we did not help Him either. I knew there was only one thing to do to faithfully walk the path that Jesus had laid out for me.

I invited Enos to live with me until he could get back on his feet. He laughed and declined the invitation. Apparently he was exactly where God needed him to be and wasn't planning on going anywhere until further instructions from the Big Guy. Suddenly Enos pulled a little flip mode on me. In our next several visits, he began to explain the gospel to me. He outlined specific verses for me to read to understand the kingdom of God and Jesus' second coming. Now Enos was helping me! You never know who is going to help who, when you set yourself to selflessly serving your brothers and sisters in Christ. God's plan will always keep you on your toes!

Bro in OKC

My life had fully turned around. I had my faith, a new job, new friends and a fresh perspective on life. I was praying that my brother would experience the same kind of healing and find God's path for his life. It was a longer, more drawn out process for him, but he too had a moment to know he was right where God planned for him to be.

In the summer of 2012, my brother flew out to Oklahoma City for the collegiate national wakeboarding tournament. Teams and individuals from all over the country were there and the competition was stiff. Cam had previously never made it to the second round the other years he had competed in the same tournament. With new confidence and strength that can only come through the healing power of the Father, he placed third in the entire nation!

That night as our family had a rare dinner gathering to celebrate, I was absolutely in awe by what God had done in not only my life, but in the lives of my family. My parents told me that they were planning on doing a mission trip to Haiti that fall. All my prayers for healing and new Godly initiatives in our lives were coming to fruition! The Father is faithful to those who wholly believe in Him and His everlasting love. There is no darkness that Jesus can't lift you out of!

Falling Again, Literally

You'd think by now that I would have it all figured out. God had revealed a part of His plan for my life and now that I was on board with that, things had never been better. That is true. It is also true that I still struggled with my signature sins. Each day is a battle not to fall into familiar traps and fill my life with things that will never be enough. I have diagnosed myself to have many sin problems, but there is one in particular that really separates me from God - pride.

As a human, I can't help but want to receive praise and acceptance from family, friends, coworkers and even strangers. I want people to think I'm great and I also want them to tell me how great I am. That is not healthy and basically means that you are worshiping yourself as an idol, instead of letting all the glory be for God. I started praying that God would humble me. Proceed with caution should you want to

67

pray the same, because that is a dangerous prayer! I knew that He would have no problems showing me how to die to my pride.

Since it was summer, our company had a lake day one Friday. When I found out there would be a boat, I was excited because I would get a chance to go wakeboarding. I'm not even close to being as good as Cam, but I can do a trick or two. Actually, just two. I knew in the depths of my heart where no one can see but me and God, that I really wanted to wakeboard, so I could impress people at work. I was hoping they would tell me I was awesome and want to be my friend. How lame does that sound? I knew this was a dangerous game to play, so I prayed, "Father, humble me if my pride gets in the way of Your glory."

Lake Day rolled around. I finally got the chance to wakeboard. Everyone in the company was on the shore, some swimming, some relaxing. I warmed up and threw a flip when we were out of site of everyone to see if I still had it. I barely landed, but thought, *Alright, now to throw it in front of everyone!* We circled around and I waited until I was right in front of the crowd. As I cut into the wake to throw the flip, everything felt wrong. Still, in true me-fashion, I barreled in head first in hopes of procuring my own glory. I didn't get enough air and thus crashed and burned right in front of over 70 some coworkers.

Honestly, I immediately looked up and thanked God for keeping me humble. It was an easy way for Him to rebuke me and show me that He is all powerful and in control. My pride can never defeat that. Nothing like falling in front of a crowd to inject you with a little humility!

.000000000000000001% of His Plan Revealed

How big is God's plan? We cannot even fathom it. You could try, but you will never know just how grand, how intricate, how fantastic is His plan for our lives! When you do start to see God working in your life, you can't help but praise Him. His Spirit is alive in us!

Being new to Austin, I really appreciated anyone that reached out to me. Penny was a coworker that managed one of the programs I handled in Peru. She was the first person to sit me down in her office and ask me how I *really* was. As a believer, she took the time to get to know me as a brother in Christ. She invited me to her church and shared parts of her testimony with me. She really helped to encourage me in times when I was struggling with being alone in Texas. One day, we were chatting at work and I saw a glimpse into God's crazy master plan.

Years back, Penny had volunteered for the Peace Corps in Peru. One day she had gotten into a cab for whatever reason, instead of taking the bus like she normally did. Later on, they stopped to pick up another passenger, a gringa. Penny and this gringa got to talking and exchanged emails. When Penny returned to the States, she began working in the study abroad field. Over a year later, she got an email at work from this gringa saying, "Remember me? I was wondering, is your company hiring?" It just so turns out that they were and that she was perfect for a position that had just opened up. She began working for the same company in the volunteer abroad department.

Fast-forward a year or so later. This gringa gets a call from a broken guy in Lexington, KY. He decides he will teach English in Chile. At the end of his program he gets an email from her saying there is a job opening in Austin. The gringa's name of course is Tanya! It is fascinating how God has woven us all together! Can you look back at your life and see where things just started to click? Have you ever been overwhelmed by the signs in your life directing you to a new unfamiliar territory? *God is talking to you*! Listen up! It will change your life forever!

God Speaks to Us

Why did I just share my testimony with you?
Why did I bare my pain and reveal my struggles to
you with brutal honesty? Be clear brothers and
sisters! I have experienced God alive in my life. He
talks to me in ways I never knew possible. I spent so
long trying to fill the void in my soul with the world's
empty promises. I bet you have done the same at
some point. Give that up, right now! Don't wait
another second! If you are ready for a new life with
God, the time is now. You don't need to visit a church
or preacher first, though it is always good to
completely understand what walking with Christ
entails. This decision is between you and God. If you
are ready to be made new and start listening to God's
voice, pray to Him! Here is a sample of how that
prayer might go. You can change it around to fit your
life or your struggles, because the result is the same:

"My Father in Heaven,

I can't run from You for another second. I'm tired of living the way the world wants me too. I need a new life, the kind only You can give me. Forgive me of the past sins that have put so much distance between us. I now believe that Jesus died for my sins, and that by this I am made clean. I believe that You have readied a place for me with You in Heaven. I believe that Jesus is the living son of the one true God! Give me the strength, patience and wisdom to serve You selflessly with my time here on Earth. May I be in the world, but not of it. May Your perfect will be done in my life! Thank You for Your goodness, faithfulness and endless grace.

Amen!"

You did it! Welcome to a better life my brother or sister. Don't be surprised if you start hearing God's voice in the form of chance encounters that are far too perfectly timed out to be coincidence. You must continue to work to hear His voice. If you fall back into your old life, it's like the voice gets turned down and you can no longer find His path. Rest assured, God is just waiting for you to get it together, so you can continue down His path with Him.

I will warn you that it is not an easy journey. No one's path through God ever is. Along the way you will surely stumble, but God will never leave you. Be steadfast in your prayer to Him. As in Psalm 32:8, pray for His guidance in your life. If you pray this earnestly and honestly, over time (could be seconds, could be years), His path will come before you. Rejoice when you see that path, because it means that you are a beloved child of God and your Heavenly Father is with you always!

My life will never be the same. I wake up daily thanking Jesus that this is so. Each day is a battle and only by God's grace and strength, can I persevere. If you are looking for a comfortable existence, you are probably far from His path for you. God's path almost never makes sense up front, but when you look back, you can see how it all perfectly came together.

The places He may take you to! There is truly no telling. As for my story, I couldn't even include every amazing way that God has spoken to me since I started listening. He continues to do miraculous things in my life, including presenting me with a job opportunity to live in Chile and reunite with Feña, among a long list of other things. I've learned through writing this book, that my testimony will only grow longer as the days, months and years go on. Where will His voice lead you?

Praise God,
a (working daily to be) humble servant of Jesus Christ

About the Author

God's path for Mateo led him to volunteer in Chile in 2011. As the path further unfolded, 3 years of trying to land a decent job after graduation finally came to an end. In 2012, he moved to Austin, TX to begin working with students studying in Latin America. It was there that he first penned his testimony. Blessings from above brought him back to Chile in 2013, where he continued working with students studying abroad in Valparaíso. Oh yeah, and he finally got around to finishing up the book that you are reading at this very moment. Only God knows what lies ahead . . .